THE COMPUTER ZONE

Jokes, Riddles, Tongue Twisters & "Daffynitions"

By Gary Chmielewski

Illustrated by Jim Caputo

Read Jokes. Write Jokes.

NORWOOD HOUSE PRESS

A Note to Parents and Caregivers:

As the old saying goes, "Laughter is the best medicine." It's true for reading as well. Kids naturally love humor, so why not look to their interests to get them motivated to read? The Funny Zone series features books that include jokes, riddles, word plays, and tongue twisters—all of which are sure to delight your young reader.

We invite you to share this book with your child, taking turns to read aloud to one another, practicing timing, emphasis, and expression. You and your child can deliver the jokes in a natural voice, or have fun creating character voices and exaggerating funny words. Be sure to pause often to make sure your child understands the jokes. Talk about what you are reading and use this opportunity to explore new vocabulary words and ideas. Reading aloud can help your child build confidence in reading.

Along with being fun and motivating, humorous text involves higher order thinking skills that support comprehension. Jokes, riddles, and word plays require us to explore the creative use of language, develop word and sound recognition, and expand vocabulary.

At the end of the book there are activities to help your child develop writing skills. These activities tap your child's creativity by exploring numerous types of humor. Children who write materials based on the activities are encouraged to send them to Norwood House Press for publication on our website or in future books. Please see page 24 for details.

Above all, the most important part of the reading experience is to have fun and enjoy it!

Sincerely,

Shannon Cannon

Shannon Cannon
Literacy Consultant

NORWOOD HOUSE PRESS

P.O. Box 316598 • Chicago, Illinois 60631
For information regarding Norwood House Press, please visit our website at:
www.norwoodhousepress.com or call 866-565-2900.

Editor: Jessy McCulloch
Designer: Design Lab

Library of Congress Cataloging-in-Publication Data:
Chmielewski, Gary, 1946–
  The computer zone / by Gary Chmielewski ; illustrated by Jim Caputo.
    p. cm. — (The funny zone)
  Summary: "Book contains computer-themed jokes, tongue twisters, and "Daffynitions." Backmatter includes creative writing information and exercises. After completing the exercises, readers are encouraged to write their own jokes and submit them for web site posting and future Funny Zone editions"—Provided by publisher.
  ISBN-13: 978-1-59953-300-1 (library edition : alk. paper)
  ISBN-10: 1-59953-300-6 (library edition : alk. paper) 1.
Computers—Juvenile humor. I. Caputo, Jim. II. Title.
  PN6231.E4C47 2009
  818'.5402—dc22   2008046349

Manufactured in the United States of America

COMPUTER LAB

How does a computer order food?
Off the "Menu"!

How do you praise a computer?
Data Boy!

Are you typing any faster these days?
Yep, I'm up to ten mistakes a minute!

Why are computer systems like professional tennis players?
They're both good servers!

Dave: "Do you know you can use your computer to tell the weather?"
Gail: "How do you do that?"
Dave: "If you carry it outside and it gets wet, it's raining!"

3

Teacher: "Do you turn on your computer with your right or left hand?"
Laura: "My right hand."
Teacher: "Amazing. Most people have to use the on/off switch!"

Carla: "Doctor, my monitor is giving me a headache."
Doctor: "Why's that?"
Carla: "I keep banging my head on it!"

Chris: "Would you buy a second-hand computer?"
Russell: "No. I'm only able to type with one hand as it is!"

George: "I've been on my computer all night!"
Chase: "Don't you think you'd be more comfortable on a bed like everyone else?"

Teacher: "Look at the dirt on that computer. I want the screen cleaned so I can see my face in it."
Abe: "But then it will crack and we won't be able to use it at all!"

Brent: "In other schools, students get a choice of computers to use."
Principal Howland: "You get a choice here, too. You can use the one we've got or don't use any at all!"

4

What did one keyboard say to the other keyboard?

"You're not my type!"

Screen saver –
Computer superhero

What do baby computers call their mother and father?

Mama and *Data*!

What is a computer's favorite dance?

Disk-o!

Where does an elephant carry its laptop?

In its trunk!

How did the computer criminal get out of jail?
He pressed the "esc" (escape) key!

What's an astronaut's favorite key?
The space bar!

Where do baby computer programmers like to sit?
On your laptop!

What is a digital computer?
Someone who counts on his fingers!

The laptop was more than aware
he was treated with plenty of care.
But sometimes he sighed,
"It can't be denied,
it'd be nice if I got my own chair."

Which way did the thief go when he stole the computer?
Data-way!

What would you get if you crossed a computer programmer and an Olympic athlete?
A *disk-us* thrower!

6

What do you get if you cross a computer and a kangaroo?
I don't know what you would call it, but it would always jump to conclusions!

Why was the chicken banned from sending e-mails?
She was always using *fowl* language!

David: "Teacher, would you mind e-mailing the exam results to my parents?"
Teacher: "But I thought you don't have a computer at home?"
David: "Exactly!"

7

THIS DOES NOT COMPUTE!

Customer: "I think I've got a bug in my computer."
Technician: "Does your computer make a humming noise?"
Customer: "Yes."
Technician: "Then it must be a humbug!"

Mom: "Having trouble with your computer son?"
Brent: "Yes, the PC says it can't find my printer."
Mom: "I'm not surprised. Look how messy your room is!"

Customer: "This laptop you charged me $700 for doesn't work. You said it would be trouble free."
Jim: "It is. I charged you $700 for the laptop, but you're getting all the trouble for free!"

Steve: "What's wrong with your computer?"
Gary: "Myspacebarseemstobestuck!"

Computer Geek: "Do you have a cursor on your computer?"
Hannah: "I'll say. You should hear the words my dad uses when the computer breaks down!"

What should you do if your computer crashes?
Take away its driver's license!

I had a rotten day at work today.
My computer broke down and
I had to think all day!

**What do tired computer
programmers do?**
They go home and crash!

Computer viruses to watch out for:
Diet Virus—Computer quits after one *byte*.
Disney Virus—Screen starts acting Goofy.
Las Vegas Virus—Users have to turn in their chips.
Titanic Virus—Everything goes down.

If at first you don't succeed
... call it version 1.0.

What ailment do computers get most often?
Slipped disk!

Why did the computer sneeze?
It caught a virus!

AAACHOOO!

SURFING THE NET

Why did the computer need glasses?
To improve its web *sight*!

What is the best kind of computer bug?
Spiders because they make the best web sites!

Why don't fish use computers?
They're afraid of getting stuck on the net!

Computer helpline: "How may I help you?"
Emily: "Every time I log on to the seven dwarfs' website my computer screen goes snow white ..."

What do builders use to make their websites?
.Com-crete!

Why did the skunk redesign his website?
Everyone said it stunk!

What's a computer's favorite sport?
Surfing!

Why do witches never get website addresses wrong?
They are very good at **spell**ing!

PE Teacher: "Why did you kick that ball straight at the school computer?"
Tania: "You told me to put it in the net!"

Have you seen the new dalmatian website?
No, I haven't spotted it yet!

Have you seen the new ruler website?
Yes, and other people are going to great lengths to use it!

Have you seen the new boxing website?
Yes, it really knocked me out!

Why do you keep going back to that fishing website?
I'm hooked!

How do train engineers find information on the internet?
They use a search engine!

Have you seen the new fishing website?
No, I heard it's not online yet!

Have you used the new mountain website?
Yes, and you must take a peak at it!

Dad: "Do you want some help using the internet, son?"
Matt: "No thanks, Dad. I can muck it up all by myself!"

14

Jackie: "Since you've discovered the internet, you never pay any attention to me."
James: "Who said that?"

Lisa: "I think I'm spending too much time on the internet. I'm beginning to see spots in front of my eyes."
Tina: "Have you seen an eye doctor?"
Lisa: "No, just the spots!"

Steve: "I never thought that the internet was very useful, but lately I've changed my mind."
Gary: "Let's hope this new one works better than the last one!"

Fern: "I hear you've been tracing your ancestors on the internet."
John: "Yes, and it's a mammoth task!"

Principal Howland: "I hope you're not one of those pupils who spends all day on the internet and doesn't get any exercise."
Javier: "Oh, no. Sometimes I sit around watching TV and don't get any exercise there either!"

Why do beavers spend so much time on the internet?

They never want to *log* off!

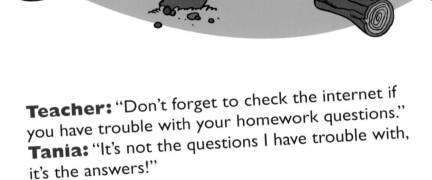

Teacher: "Don't forget to check the internet if you have trouble with your homework questions."
Tania: "It's not the questions I have trouble with, it's the answers!"

Did you hear about the geek who almost drowned?

He was surfing the web and got bumped off!

How can you learn ballet dancing on the internet?

By using the tutu-torial!

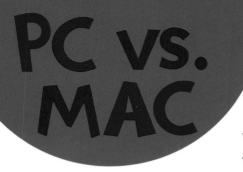

PC VS. MAC

What do computer geeks eat for dessert?
Apple pie a la modem!

Why did the lady go to the drapery store?
Her computer had *Windows*!

Why do computer teachers never get sick?
Because an *Apple* a day keeps the doctor away!

What home computer grows on trees?
An *Apple*!

Why wouldn't the cleaning lady operate a computer?
She didn't do *Windows*!

Why did the computer catch a cold?
It forgot to close the *Windows*!

Why did the computer whiz bring a computer to school?
Her mother told her to give an *Apple* to the teacher!

WRONG ADDRESS!

Have you used the new www.topsecret.com yet?
If I have, do you think I'll tell you?

Have you used www.ancienthistory.com yet?
Yes, but it was a very long time ago!

Have you used the new www.tomatosauce.com yet?
No, I'll *ketchup* with it later!

Have you used the new www.lockeddrawer.com yet?
Yes, but it was very hard to get into!

Have you used www.flea.com yet?
No, but I'm itching to find it!

Have you used the new www.needleinahaystack.com yet?
No, it's taking quite awhile to find!

Have you used www.quasimodo.com yet?
I'm not quite sure but it rings a bell!

Have you seen the new www.square.com?
No, I haven't got around to using it yet!

Have you used the new www.amnesia.com yet?
Sorry, I just can't remember that one!

Have you used www.boomerang.com yet?
Yes, and I keep returning to it!

Have you seen www.brokenglass.com?
Yes, but I don't think it's all it's cracked up to be!

What do you get if you type www.abcdefghijklmnopqrstuvwxyz.com on your keyboard?
A sore finger!

19

A HARD DRIVE

Where are delinquent disk drives sent?
To boot camp!

What's a computer's sign of old age?
Loss of memory!

How did the computers afford a vacation?
They all **chip**ped in!

What happens when a dirty computer dies?
It *bytes* the dust!

What do computer programmers like with their hamburgers?
Chips!

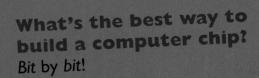

What's the best way to build a computer chip?
Bit by *bit*!

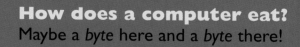

How does a computer eat?
Maybe a *byte* here and a *byte* there!

Why was the computer good at golf?
It had a good hard drive!

Where do computers keep their money?
In memory banks!

What animals help computers to run?
Rams!

Geek: "How many bytes are in your software program?"
Jason: "I'll let you know as soon as I've finished eating it!"

Why was the computer so angry?
It had a *chip* on its shoulder!

Why did the computer fall asleep?
It was tired from a hard drive!

Why was Count Dracula hanging around the computer?
He was trying to get a *byte*!

What does a computer do when it gets hungry?
It gets a *byte* to eat!

What do you get if a tarantula sits on your computer?
A spider *byte*!

WRITING JOKES CAN BE AS MUCH FUN AS READING THEM!

A limerick is a little poem that is meant to be witty or funny. It is five lines long with a very distinctive rhythm and rhyme pattern. The last words of the first, second and fifth lines must rhyme with each other. The last words in the third and fourth lines need to rhyme with each other too, but they do not need to rhyme with the words from the other lines. Here is an example from page 6:

> The **lap**top was **more** than a**ware**
> he was **treat**ed with **plen**ty of **care**.
> But **some**times he **sighed**,
> "It **can't** be de**nied**,
> it'd be **nice** if I **got** my own **chair**."

The rhythm in lines one, two and five have three beats (beats are sounds that are stressed and are bolded here). Lines three and four have only two beats. For example, if you read line one aloud, you will hear how you stress lap, more, and -ware. Not only is it funny that the laptop is tired of sitting on laps, but the rhyming and rhythm of the limerick make it fun and funny to say.

YOU TRY IT!

An easy way to get started is to think of a boy's or girl's name that has one syllable (Tim, Jill, Jack, Gail, etc.). Use it in a sentence such as, "There once was a young (boy/girl) named ___." Then, make a list of words that rhyme with the last word in the first line and write a sentence that ends with a word from this list.

Just think of it as writing a story. To write lines three and four, ask yourself what comes next? What could happen? Finally, you just need your fifth line, taking care to rhyme the last word of the limerick with the last words in lines one and two.

Here is an example of what you could write using the name Gail:

> There once was a young girl named Gail
> who went hiking along an old trail.
> She thought she felt rain,
> but it caused her such pain,
> she looked up and then saw it was hail!

Ideas for limericks can come from just about anywhere – your city, your name, animals, sports teams, the choices are almost endless. Impress your friends, family, even your teachers with your own limerick.

SEND US YOUR JOKES!

Pick out the best limerick that you created and send it to us at Norwood House Press. We will publish it on our website — organized according to grade level, the state you live in, and your first name.

Selected jokes might also appear in a future special edition book, *Kids Write in the Funny Zone*. If your joke is included in the book, you and your school will receive a free copy.

Here's how to send the jokes to Norwood House Press:

1) Go to www.norwoodhousepress.com.
2) Click on the **Enter the Funny Zone** tab.
3) Select and print the joke submission form.
4) Fill out the form, include your joke, and send to:
> The Funny Zone
> Norwood House Press
> PO Box 316598
> Chicago, IL 60631

Here's how to see your joke posted on the website:

1) Go to www.norwoodhousepress.com.
2) Click on the **Enter the Funny Zone** tab.
3) Select **Kids Write in the Funny Zone** tab.
4) Locate your grade level, then state, then first name.
> If it's not there yet check back again.